ANIMAL
TALK

First edition for the United States, Canada,
and the Philippines published 1991
by Barron's Educational Series, Inc.

© Copyright by Aladdin Books, Ltd 1991

Design David West Children's Book Design
Illustrations Kate Taylor
Text Anita Ganeri
Picture research Angela Graham

Created and designed by
N.W. Books
28 Percy Street
London W1P 9FF

All inquiries should be addressed to:
Barron's Educational Series, Inc.
250 Wireless Boulevard
Hauppauge, NY 11788

International Standard Book No. 0-8120-6239-6

Library of Congress Catalog Card No. 91-9966

Library of Congress Cataloging-in Publication Data

Ganeri, Anita, 1961-
Talk / by Anita Ganeri : illustrated by Kate Taylor.
p.   cm. -- (Animal questions and answers)
Summary: Introduces the many different ways in
which animals communicate with each other,
including different sounds, scents, movement, and
color, in a question and answer format.
ISBN 0-8120-6239-6
1. Animal communication--Miscellanea--Juvenile
literature. [1. Animal communication--Miscellanea.
2. Questions and answers.] I. Taylor, Kate, ill. II. Title.
III. Series.
QL778.G36   1991
591.59--dc20   91-9966   CIP   AC

Printed in Belgium
1234   987654321

QUESTIONS AND ANSWERS ABOUT

ANIMAL TALK

Barron's

New York • Toronto

How do animals talk?

We use words to talk to each other. But other animals cannot speak with words. Instead they have many different ways of talking. Have you ever wished you could talk to animals and find out more about them? This book will help you learn more about the many special languages which animals use to communicate.

How do animals use sign language?

A moth makes a tasty snack for a hungry bird. Moths cannot tell the birds to go away so some moths use special signs instead. They have huge spots on their back wings. The spots look like eyes. By flashing their false eyes at the birds, the moths frighten them off.

Can animals use human sign language?

Koko, a gorilla, can talk in human sign language. She knows about 1,000 words. She makes the sign for "bad" when she has been naughty.

Which birds are the best mimics?

Some birds copy the songs of others. Warblers are some of the best mimics. They can sing the songs of over 80 other types of birds.

Which animals can talk like humans?

Parrots, parakeets and mynah birds are very good at copying what people say. An African gray parrot, called Prudle, could say about 800 words. Scientists believe that these birds don't know what they are talking about. But a parrot, called Alex, did learn to say "no" if it didn't want to be picked up.

Which animals howl at the moon?

Wolves are famous for their ghostly howling. But they don't really howl at the moon. Wolves live in packs. They howl to keep in touch with each other and to tell other packs where they are. When one wolf starts howling, the others soon join in.

Which animals howl in chorus?

Howler monkeys howl to protect their territory. If another group of monkeys comes too close, the two groups howl in chorus. Then the strangers go away. The howling can be heard 10 miles away.

Which animal laughs?

Hyenas sometimes sound as if they are laughing wildly. They suddenly burst into fits of noisy, cackling laughter. This is just one of the sounds they use for talking to each other. Apart from laughing they also growl, yelp and grunt.

Why do some animals grin?

We grin if we feel happy or think something is funny. Chimpanzees can look as if they are grinning too. But if they show their teeth they are not happy. They are probably afraid or about to attack.

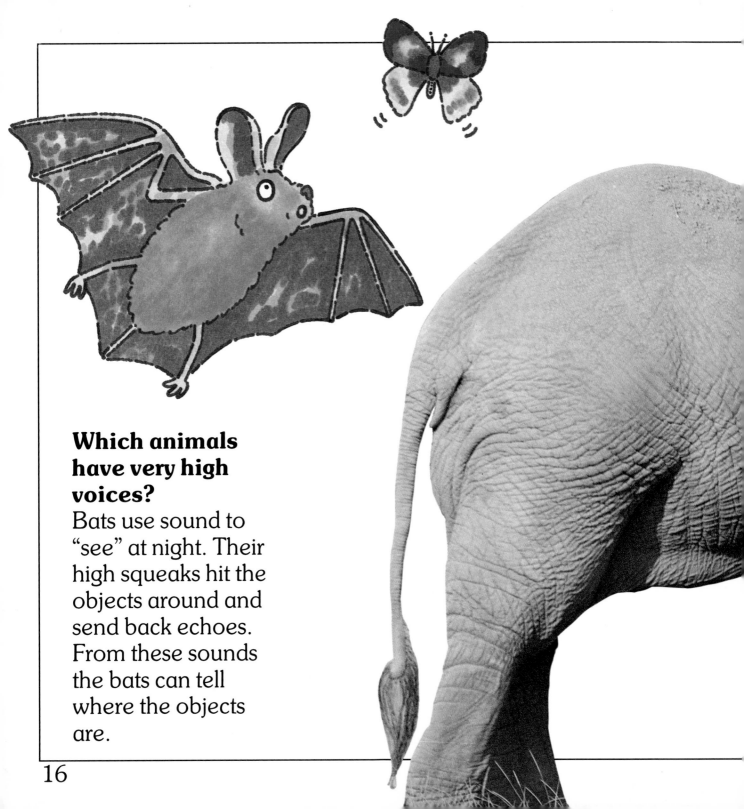

Which animals have very high voices?

Bats use sound to "see" at night. Their high squeaks hit the objects around and send back echoes. From these sounds the bats can tell where the objects are.

16

Which animal has a very deep voice?

Elephants sometimes look for food among thick bushes. They make a deep growling sound to let the others know where they are. If the elephants can see each other easily, they don't need to growl.

Do animals talk underwater?

Many sea animals don't talk at all. But dolphins use lots of sounds to talk underwater. They grunt, squeal and bark to show if they are happy, angry or excited. Each dolphin also has its own special whistle. This is its name. It tells the others who it is.

Which animal has the loudest voice?

Whales talk to each other miles across the oceans. They need loud voices to carry long distances. A blue whale's voice is louder than a jet airplane.

Why do birds sing in the morning?

Have you ever been woken up by the sound of the birds singing? Birds sing to each other instead of talking. They sing to keep in touch. Birds sing in the morning to tell other birds to keep away from their homes. The morning air is very still. Their songs can be heard a long way away.

Which animal sings with its wings?
Male crickets don't really sing. They rub their front wings together to make a chirping sound. A grasshopper sings by rubbing its back leg over its front wing.

Which animals send smell messages?

Many animals use smells to talk to others. The skunk is one of the smelliest animals. If an enemy gets too close, the skunk squirts an oily, yellow liquid which smells terrible. The enemy makes a speedy getaway.

How many smells can an animal make?

Tropical tree ants make ten different smells. By mixing the smells up, they can send about 50 different messages, such as "Danger" or "Food this way."

Which animals thump on the ground to raise an alarm?

Rabbits live in burrows under the ground. But they have to come out to look for food. They are always on the lookout for danger. They don't want to be eaten themselves by other hungry animals. If one of the rabbits sees an enemy it thumps on the ground with its big back feet. The other rabbits dash back to safety in their burrows.

Which animal has an alarm in its tail?

Rattlesnakes are very dangerous if they are disturbed. They coil up and rattle their tails in the air. This rattling sound scares enemies away.

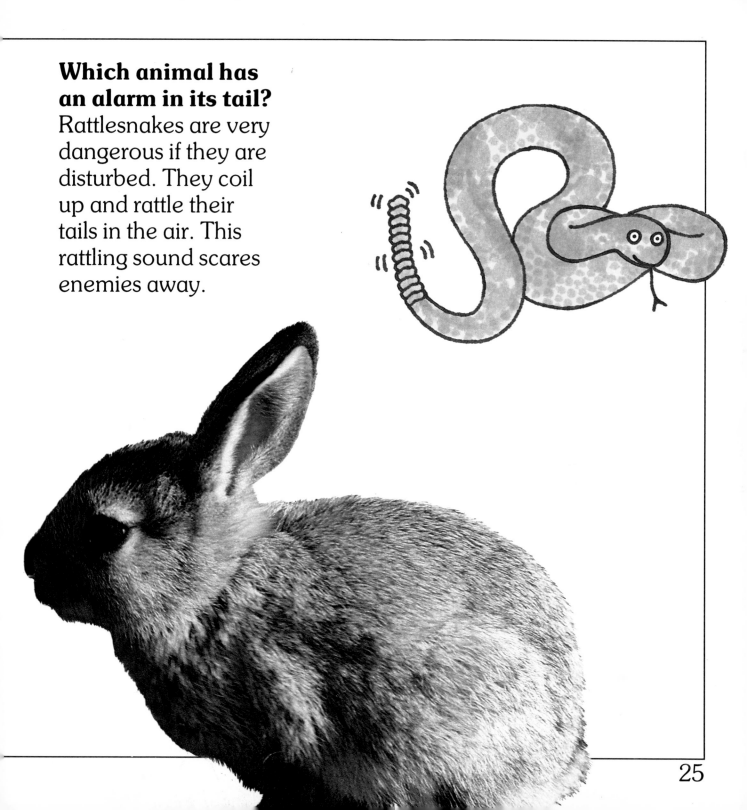

Which animals kiss when they meet?

Prairie dogs live together in huge groups. When two prairie dogs meet, they kiss to find out if they know each other. If they do, they groom each other and go off to feed. If one of the prairie dogs is a stranger, he is chased away.

Which animals dance?

Honeybees visit flowers to collect syrupy nectar. They take it back to their hive to make honey. Then they do an amazing type of dance. The dance tells the other bees exactly where to fly to find the best flowers.

Which animals use flags to talk?

Some animals use parts of their bodies like flags to send messages. A male anole lizard has a floppy flap of brightly-colored skin under his chin. It is called a flag. He usually keeps it folded up. To send messages, he stretches the skin out and waves it like a flag. He uses his flag to scare off enemies and to attract a female partner.

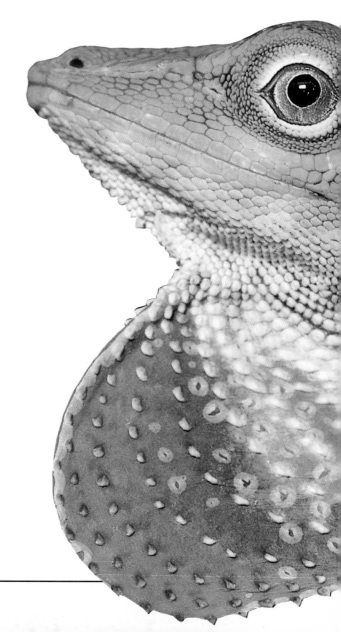

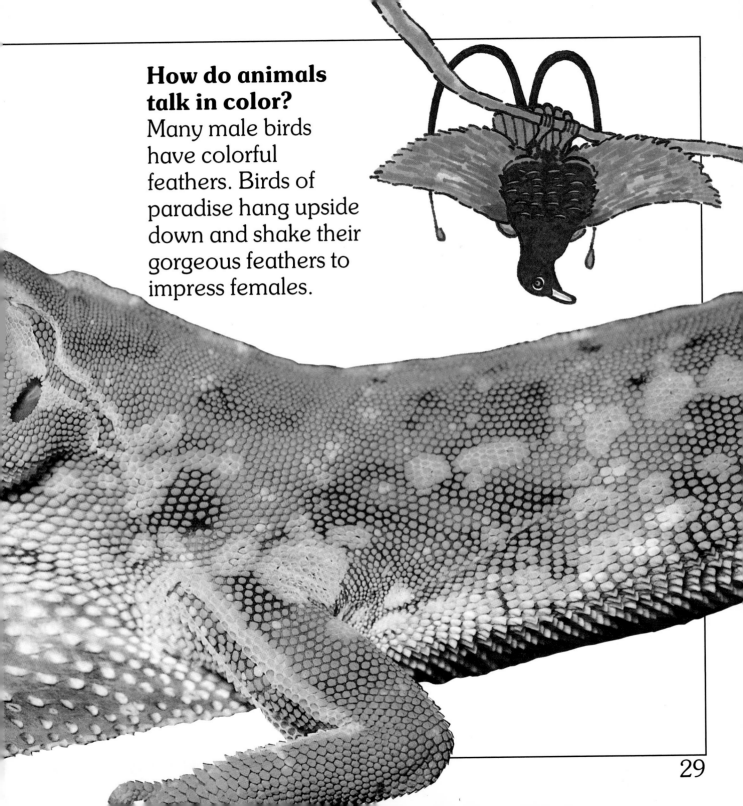

How do animals talk in color?

Many male birds have colorful feathers. Birds of paradise hang upside down and shake their gorgeous feathers to impress females.

29

Index

Photographs
Cover Roger Vlitos; pages 5, 7, 10/11, 12, 17, 20, 23, 24, 29
left: Bruce Coleman; 9, 27: Survival Anglia; page 13: Science
Picture Library; page 14: Frank Lane Picture Library; pages 18,
25: Planet Earth.